See Saw

A Series of Poems on Art

Adrian Buckner

Leafe Press

Published by Leafe Press
Nottingham, England.
www.leafepresspoetry.com

Text copyright © Adrian Buckner, 2023. All rights reserved.

Cover artwork and design copyright © Bob Moulder, 2023.

ISBN: 978-1-7397213-5-0

Lytton (Strachey) was a great reader. Holroyd (Michael, his biographer) tends to describe this as idleness, an attitude which Lytton himself shared. But reading is not idleness – any more than listening to music or looking at pictures – it is the passive, receptive side of civilization without which the active and creative would be meaningless. It is the immortal spirit of the dead realized within the bodies of the living. It is sacramental.

Stephen Spender *Journals 1939 – 1983.*
4th January 1980

Giotto

The Entry into Jerusalem, c.1305

I am a smiling donkey
I am practically giggling
With the Good News

When the golden age arrives
For children's illustrated books

I will trot from this fresco
Onto those pages

And wreathe the unlettered
In smiles again

Fra Angelico

*The Decapitation of St Cosmas and St Damian,
c.1440*

When I am called to account at The Hague
I will say I was obeying orders
Like the three lads on crowd control rota

Look to the front row for the guilty
The self-absolving gestures

The more in sorrow than anger
Exporters of rational governance

Through a swing of the sword
A drone strike in the desert

Ghirlandaio

Old Man with a Young Boy, 1490

No need to look out there
My dearest boy
Ideals and nature are still trading

Have eyes only for me
As I have eyes only for you

Touching
They will call it

And go on to write their novels
Their brief lyrical poems

Raphael
The Madonna of the Pinks, 1506

Mother and I
Are in agreement
This artist knocks our socks off

She the ur-serene
I no longer pug ugly

So at ease are we
I am tempted to tease

Yes mama it's a lovely carnation
Can John come round now?

Cranach
Adam and Eve, 1526

Why thank you Eve
An Apple as red as your hair
As delicious as ourselves

Well it is 1526
I'm meant to think for myself

No obvious devils or haloes about
Nature looking natural

Knowledge is so tempting
And soon enough apples will be falling from trees

Gentileschi
Susanna and the Elders, 1610

Be in no doubt Susanna
We mean to invade
More than your personal space

Behind beyond
In front of you

The bitter breath
Of human slander

Will blow across
A mountainscape of malice

Velasquez
The Adoration of the Magi, 1619

I've got my eyes on you Melchior
And though this be our shining time
I think I'll keep them there

Mother is too polite to say
But on balance we prefer Shepherds

Knowing as we do how things
Tend to turn out with guys like you

With your wisdom
And your gold

Rembrandt
A child being taught to walk, 1656

      Here
Let me show you
All you can neither see nor hear

The entire expression of a girl
With her back to you

The exact sweet note
Of her father's beckoning persuasion

The level in the maid's pail
      There

Vermeer
Study of a Young Woman, 1665-7

When I come to the party in New York
Be honest about what you see
Be clear about your feelings

Two hundred years of disregard
Must count for something

I come with nothing behind me
I waited for you to know

The harmony of my discretion
The splendour of his slowness

Chardin
The House of Cards, 1736-37

We made our own entertainment back then
One Saturday night I reached
Level eight of *Palladian Manor*

Ached in my breeches all Sunday
To tell Gustave

Ah Gustave
My frenemy my bromance

So grieved to hear you've reached
The last level of *Syphilitic Gambling Den*

Hokusai
Thirty-six Views of Mount Fuji, c.1831

Thirty-six
Isn't the half of it
A mountain

Like a Cathedral
Like a water lily

Like a sunflower
Like another mountain

Just cannot stop
Being painted

Perov
Portrait of Fyodor Dostoevsky, 1872

I am not posed in the darkness
I look from the dark
Into a man's soul

I am all fingers and thumbs
Attempting a prayer

When Petersburg is starved and frozen
It will refuse to die

The libraries will stay open
Men will look into my books

Morisot
The Cradle, 1872

When my daughter wakes
Her eyes will spring open to the world
She will make one leap into the morning

Like the men I know
Their bars their streets their far flung fields

Me? I will be in the park today
Hunting butterflies with the older children

Awake to the whole world
Is that what they mean by *feminine delicacy?*

Schmidt-Rotluff
Flowering Trees, 1909

I left her sleeping
In the light and airy room
The window curtain pulsing with the breeze

The tiny travels of her breath
On the terrain of the duvet

I walked into the lane
Past the glittering tulip tree

My heart's flame
My heart's ease

Marc (to Nash)
Little Blue Horse, 1912

I will not be around Paul
To gaze across
The new world they are making

What can an artist do
What can a man do

Except place his own
Little Blue Horse

In the landscape blaze
Of his mind?

Duchamp
Fountain, 1917

My name is Rachel Mutt
I work from four to eight three times a day
Nine days a week fifteen months of the year

Cleaning lavatories in an Institute of Higher Education
In the English Midlands

Life has dealt me seven truckloads of shit
Leaving me with nothing but pride in my work

Ignoring the framed sheet above the hand dryers
I signed today my very own piece of Art

Gwen John
Young Woman Holding a black cat, 1920

I am an unknown female sitter
Arrested in my personal pandemic
Of loneliness

In one hundred years from now
There will be seven billion cats on computers

One for every soul
On the planet

Mine will be forever black
And twisting in my arms

Hopper
Automat, 1927

He just upped and left
She tells me
No word   no hope

The foam on her coffee
Dries to a Hokusai wave

I too   leave her
Make into the night

Pass a lone treadmiller
In the wide glass of the all-night gym

Dufy
The Avenue du Bois de Boulogne, 1928

All the leaves in Raoul's tree
Are all the birds
About to fly

A few have fallen
On the Avenue du Bois

Where Ladies and Gentlemen know
The delicacy of Raoul's hand

And have the good manners
Not to sit in his chairs

Lowry
Seascape, 1952

You don't know much about art
But you know what you like
Or thought you did

Tempted was I
To put a little black dog on the shore?

Perhaps a shivering family
Enduring an awkward exchange?

I'll give you a maybe black bird
Under a maybe celestial arch

Rothko (to Leonardo)

I'm grieving Leonardo
Your Last Supper won't last
What were you thinking in front of the dry wall?

Shiny clutter will fill the void
I've seen it in my own time

My own calamity
Why did I agree that commission?

So much passing through
So much chatter

Leonardo (to Rothko)

We all make mistakes Mark
So my fresco fades
You have five centuries to love it

So much else is lost
So much destroyed in a moment

Born into your time I would be maddened
With grief and ideas

Here with you I can gaze on your murals
High above those rich bastards in Hell

The Last Supper, 1494-8
The Seagram Murals, 1959

Morandi
Still life, 1960

We have gathered again
On the still pond
Me and the six little ones

My eldest is most like me
Benign old fusspot

The others love to be with and near him
As they love to be with and near me

We have no desire to swim away
From Giorgio's house

Hilton
Boat, 1974

My six-year-old could have done that
And he did
One day when I was all at sea

Oh my darling six-year-old
Please never stop

Trying to set me right
Upon the waves

I will always let you down
Nearly always let you down
.

Rae
I need gentle conversations, 2012

I am the paint
The strokes the shapes every lush surprise
On a work of art by Fiona Rae

Charmed to my toes when she stood back from me
To give me this name

What the world needs now
Is gentle conversations

It's the only thing
There's never been a picture of

Notes

p 16   Perov
"Frozen and silent, Leningrad refused to die; the libraries stayed open."
Neal Ascherson. Episode 11, *Red Star: The Soviet Union 1941-43*. *The World at War*. Thames Television. 1973.

p17   Morisot
The Butterfly Hunt was painted by Morisot in 1874

p19   Marc
Franz Marc was killed at Verdun in 1916.
We Are Making a New World was painted by Paul Nash in 1918

p 25   Leonardo (to Rothko)
"I hope to ruin the appetite of every son of a bitch who eats in that room"
Mark Rothko, 1959 (in conversation with John Fischer, publisher of *Harper's Magazine*).

p28   Rae
What The World Needs Now   David/Bacharach 1965

List of Works:

Giotto	*The Entry into Jerusalem, c.1305*
Fra Angelico	*The Decapitation of St Cosmas and St Damian, c.1440*
Ghirlandaio	*Old Man with a Young Boy, 1490*
Raphael	*The Madonna of the Pinks, 1506*
Cranach	*Adam and Eve, 1526*
Gentileschi	*Susanna and The Elders, 1610*
Velasquez	*The Adoration of the Magi, 1619*
Rembrandt	*A child being taught to walk, 1656*
Vermeer	*Study of a Young Woman, 1665-7*
Chardin	*The House of Cards, 1736-7*
Hokusai	*Thirty-six Views of Mount Fuji, c.1831*
Perov	*Portrait of Fyodor Dostoevsky, 1872*
Morisot	*The Cradle, 1872*
Schmidt-Rotluff	*Flowering Trees, 1909*
Marc (to Nash)	*Little Blue Horse, 1912*
Duchamp	*Fountain, 1917*
Gwen John	*Young Woman Holding a black cat, 1920*
Hopper	*Automat, 1927*
Dufy	*The Avenue du Bois de Boulogne, 1928*
Lowry	*Seascape, 1952*
Leonardo (to Rothko)	*The Last Supper, 1494-8;*
Rothko (to Leonardo)	*The Seagram Murals, 1959*
Morandi	*Still Life, 1960*
Hilton	*Boat, 1974*
Rae	*I need gentle conversations, 2012*

Acknowledgements

Duchamp has previously appeared on *Litter* and the *AUB competition anthology* website.
Giotto and Vermeer have previously appeared on *Litter*.
Hopper was first published in *Cyphers*
Thanks to Bob Moulder for his cover artwork and design.

www.ingramcontent.com/pod-product-compliance
Lightning Source LLC
Chambersburg PA
CBHW042337040426
42446CB00021B/3482